The Seasons Tell Me...

Horia Ajheer

Presentation by *BookLeaf Publishing*
Web: www.bookleafpub.com
E-mail: info@bookleafpub.com

ISBN : 9789358364903

First edition 2021

This book is dedicated to all of you,
whose pieces I found,
and keep on finding.

Acknowledgement

I would like to take this chance to express my gratitude those around me who have always supported me and encouraged me to write and keep writing. It did not matter how many times I gave up, it did not matter that some didn't even enjoy or understand poetry, nor did it matter how unhappy I was with my own progress. They always had my back and gave me confidence to take this important step.

I'm very grateful to my family, my friends.

Thank you for believing in me.

Preface

I have always been someone who kept the things I wrote to myself, and a small group of close friends and family. Writing to publish was a big step for me. For this book I depended on my senses and memories to reminisce and reflect on life. I hope that you as the reader will be able to find meaning you can relate to in my words.

Whispers

It is the sighs of the wind,
that made me take note of the message
beyond your spoken words.
The underlying whispers pleading
to be heard,
to be understood.
I took a long time;
I apologise.
But I hear you,
I see you,
I feel you,
I will answer you
with whispers of my own.

Starry sky

It is in the glimmer of the starry sky
that I see your eyes.
How they gaped at far away lights
in the blue sky
turning darker by the second,
studying every aspect carefully.

It was then that I realised
how I am grateful for
your ability to show me
how much this world has to offer;

how you always manage to
find joy in new things so easily;
how you share your vast world
with me, allowing me
into a world of wonder;

how you always manage
to draw me out of the safety of my shell
even when I hole myself up well;
how when you acquaint
me with the novelties within you,
I notice your excitement

as if you are experiencing
it all for the first time again.

And every shimmer in this, now navy sky,
represents, for me, the novelties
that you brought with you into my life.

Words

It was the shattering thunder that
reminded me of your words,
they stung and stabbed me
in places of my soul
that I thought I had protected well.
My defenses did not hold up against this
venomous weapon,
and I was left exposed, vulnerable.
I guess that is exactly why
they left such deeply engraved scars.
And it is also the reason
I chose to grow without you.

Summer

The Seasons tell me stories
they have been burning to tell.
It just happened to be me
they took under their spell.

Summer taught me
that one's way of life can end abruptly,
that the aftermath of loss
are scars and cavity.
Scars blooming and staining
the very core of one's being;
a cavity left by the presence
which once was,
but is no longer.

One moment you feel the burning
of frustration, of anger, of tears.

The next you feel
the lightness and coldness
of loneliness, of longing, of your fears.

Summer taught me
that one's life can change suddenly,
with or without warning.
And you find yourself longing
for different times.

And eventually you find yourself in
Autumn.

Warmth

It is when the sand at the shore
hugs my feet that I am reminded
of your presence in my world.
The sensation of the warmth
my toes have sunk in and the occasional
sharp prick of a pebble or shell
resemble the experiences and history we
share.

I have always wanted to ask you...
When you looked at yourself,
what was it you saw?
Do you notice everything that I do
when I look at you?

Because when I used to look at you,
I saw your brave steps skipping through
a day, a rough morning,
a fulfilling afternoon,
and a serene evening.
And a week passed soon.

I saw the smile in your eyes
whenever you talked,

eager to share pieces
of yourself with the world.

I wonder what it is that you see.
If only we could go back,
then I would gather the courage
to ask you to tell me.

The night

There is light in the night.
Light people have stopped
to care about or to even notice;
light that has been overshadowed
by pollution of manmade ones.

But once I took notice of the brilliant map
reflecting the universe
on our curtain of dark
I discovered pieces of myself
and pieces of my world,
new and old.

These lights taken for granted,
I acknowledge it all,
I appreciate you.

Drops of the rain

It is in the drops of the rain
that I see the things
that define the difference
between you and me.
You,
a beautiful dome shaped bud of a drop,
capturing the reflection
of a remarkable sparkle of light,
appear to be
standing strong and charismatic.
Me?
I'm a fading streak
running down the window,
leaving a weak trail of my presence;
soon to evaporate and disappear entirely.
This is the perception I had
of my admiration for you,
and my impression of myself
when I compared myself to you.
And I,
I wonder what the world is like through
your eyes.

Autumn

The Seasons tell me stories
they have been burning to tell.
It just happened to be me
they took under their spell.

Autumn taught me a wise lesson.
Everything comes to an end,
making space for something new,
something different.
It takes time and effort
to reach acceptance,
to allow the drought of denial
to be soaked by the rain of realisation.
Though it is difficult to acknowledge
the emptiness of that which has ended,
I am aware that the void
can be filled once more.

All I need is courage,
 the courage to not shy
away from being drenched,
to be ready for the flood of emotions
and allow myself to cry.

What helps me to move forward,
is knowing that the rain will become
a blanket of white in Winter.
In winter I will have courage,
I hope.

The trail

I was told that some notice the drop
at the end of the trail
Curious.
How frail.
They find themselves wondering
where it is headed;
whether it will reach
the edge of the window.
They find themselves lost,
lost in thought;
lost in wonder;
lost in the streak
that is the trail of the curious drop that
caught their eye.

The leaves rustle

It is in the rustling of the leaves
that I hear your laughter,
as the warm gentle breeze
swirls and scatters.
A chime of joy
unique to each and every person,
and only *yours* reaches a part of me
no one has ever laid eyes on.

The vibrant tune was laced with bravery
to express a spectrum of emotions.
I can only admire the physical outlet
of all hues of your passion.
Beautiful, is the halo that envelops you
when you laugh.
And I,
I only wish that you see it too.

Wonder

It was the distant ticking of the clock
that got me to thinking.
My mind drifted
in a monologue of reflection,
trying to reason.

You end up wondering,
you couldn't even comprehend,
how you end up in certain circumstances.
You would have to settle
with the fact that you cannot
contemplate your choices.
You don't even have time to ponder;
you are only getting dragged along,
once again.
You do not really understand.
But it doesn't matter,
that you may not even have made them,
those choices
And you,
and me are just pulled in,
wondering what happened
to those choices?

Strangers

It was the way the flocks of birds
flew over the sea
that reminded me of the things unresolved
between you and me.
As they seemed to head for the moon
far above the horizon,
clouds that had filled me over time
seemed to brace for a storm.

I had never expected us
to head this way in life.
I had always thought that we
were like the flocks of fluttering wings,
headed in the same direction.
With the same ideals,
sharing the same ocean of affection.
But it seemed that that was not the case;
step by step, we headed
into directions that did not align.
Your distance
grew and kept growing until at some point
I could not even recognise your face.

And my mind was growing a void.
We were not going to be fine, were we?
We became strangers,
Didn't we?

Winter

The Seasons tell me stories
they have been burning to tell.
It just happened to be me
they took under their spell.

Winter taught me resilience
just not when it mattered most;
in ways I had not yet experienced
just not in the way I had hoped.
The thick blanket of white
was holding the world in its bold embrace.
Winter had a plan in mind.
The plan to renew what had gotten erased,
and to preserve what Autumn could save.
It was in Winter
when I found the resolution,
in obtaining something new
after I what I had lost in Autumn.
Though I was hoping to find courage,
I found myself accepting my emotions
and my feelings as they were,

I made peace with my mind and heart
being at odds sometimes, and I learned
that I was calmed and encouraged,
by that new peace I found.

I started to finally believe,
that Spring would help me find
the courage I was trying to achieve.

Wander

It was in the streaks of light
spread across the floor
that I felt like the realisation finally hit.

The sun peeked through the windows
leaving their marks on the green carpet
and showed off the the scenery outdoors.

I could clearly hear the voice inside me
it was nervous, shaken, unsure as it spoke.

"And there you are,
wandering into a whole new world.
Everything sounds different,
you hear gibberish around you.
Everything looks different,
the buildings, the streets,
the boats, the stores.
Everyone looks different,
not tan, but white; not dark, but blonde."
And when I came here,
They were bewildered.
"What are they doing?"
is what they wondered.

And I,
I was met with looks I couldn't place.
Now,
Now I recognise them.
At some point,
you grow painfully aware of them.
Disdain, disapproval, disgust.
These looks, caused by ignorance.

Because you don't know.
How could you know when
you won't open your eyes.
The pain I, we, go through;
all of the losses we have faced,
and still face to this very day;
what runs through our minds
every time,
every single time
we get asked: Who?
Who are you to come into my home,
when you're,
uninvited, unaccepted, unreasonable?
Who do you think you are,
claiming to live here when you don't
belong, blend in, bend?

Why do you think you can stay?
Just disappear, go away.

But I won't, conform to
those wills and wishes.

Hail

It was in the restless rattling of the hail
that I realised my mind
had finally decided;
it was determination that prevailed.
I braced myself for the impact,
the consequences of the actions
that I would take and the result
of the events that would unfold.

I convinced myself that I was ready,
though the bubble of fear was left untold.
Was there an easy way to do and say,
was there an answer
to these questions burning within?

Bright

It was in the glistening sunlight
on the surface of the sea
that I saw that you were so bright.
How bright your smile was, though timid
radiating a calm joy;
how brightly your eyes
twinkled with spirit.

You look like you could take on
everything in those moments
in a way that my mind whirled
with the belief that if I followed
you, that I'd get there too.
Would I be let into your world?

Spring

The Seasons tell me stories
they have been burning to tell.
It just happened to be me
they took under their spell.

Spring taught me
that patience gets rewarded,
maybe not in the way I had expected it,
maybe not when I thought I needed it
the most.
Spring brought me greens and yellows
to replace the bare, dull grey
that Winter left behind,
eventually joined by many other hues.

I could hear the white noise of nature,
of life awakening, and smell the breeze
that tingled my nose
and overwhelmed my lungs
with its crips freshness.
It was in Spring when I learned
how strong I could be;
and it was in spring when
I allowed myself to ... just be.

Spring taught me
that patience is rewarded,
when I found the courage to allow myself
to believe that I deserved it.

The spring breeze

It was in the humble warmth
of the spring breeze
that I felt your embrace.

The comfort I find in your presence;
your infallible words of wisdom and care
encourage me to dare.
The hold that promised me,
the voice that assured me,
the smile that endorsed me,
the eyes that seem to adore me,

They all tell me one and the same.
You can take the universe;
it is and always be yours to claim.

The day

There are shadows in the day.
When everyone focusses on
the light, the bright,
the warmth, the swarms
of people in the day.

But when the sun is out,
it's the shadows that I see;
the lonely, the nobody,
the unseen, the serene
scenery of diversity,
seemingly undesired.

I see all of it,
I see all of you.

Story

It was a field of daisies
that made me reflect on myself one day.
A single daisy missing one petal
had caught my attention.
What is your story, little daisy;
what took your leaf away?
Is it a story you even want to share,
are you willing to lay out
your heart and soul?
But wait, stop, is it even fair?
To drive you into a corner
and losing control.
It was my curiosity that caused me
to not take you into consideration,
and made me be
a version of myself that I loathe.
I'm sorry, little daisy.
Can you forgive me?